914.415

D0492623

FIESTA!

Ireland

Lorien Kite

W
FRANKLIN WATTS
NEW YORK • LONDON • SYDNEY

First published 1998

Franklin Watts
96 Leonard Street
London EC2A 4RH

0 7496 2938 X

Dewey Decimal Classification Number: 394.2

Marshall Cavendish Limited
Editorial staff
Editorial Director: Ellen Dupont
Art Director: Joyce Mason
Designer: Norma Martin
Editor: Tessa Paul
Sub-Editors: Susan Janes, Judy Fovargue
Production: Craig Chubb

Crafts devised and created by Susan Moxley
Music arrangements by Harry Boteler
Photographs by Bruce Mackie
Consultant: Patricia O'Donoghue

Printed in Italy

Adult supervision advised for all crafts and recipes
particularly those involving sharp instruments and heat.

CONTENTS

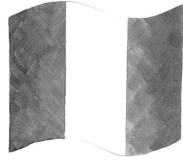

IRELAND

At the western edge of Europe, Ireland looks out across 1,200 kilometres of ocean to North America.

▲ **Potatoes** are probably the most popular vegetable in Ireland. People say that Sir Walter Raleigh, the English explorer who lived from 1552-1618, was the first to bring the potato to Ireland. He discovered it on his travels in South America.

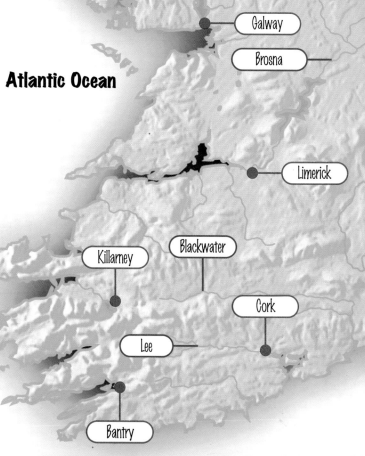

Sligo

Castlebar

Atlantic Ocean

Galway

Brosna

Limerick

Blackwater

Killarney

Lee

Cork

Bantry

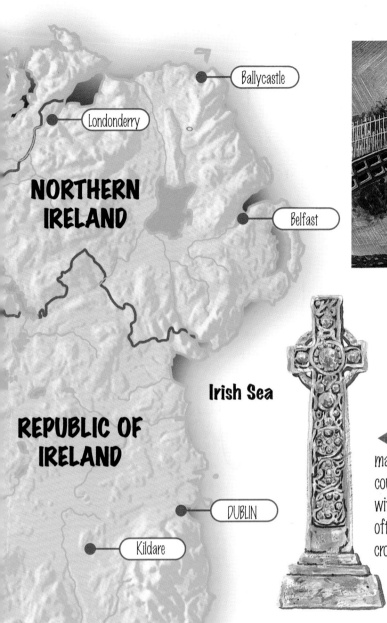

Ballycastle

Londonderry

NORTHERN IRELAND

Belfast

Irish Sea

REPUBLIC OF IRELAND

DUBLIN

Kildare

Kilkenny

Slaney

Waterford

Wexford

▲ **Dublin** is the capital of the Irish Republic. The River Liffey (above) flows through the city and into the Irish Sea. For hundreds of years, Dublin has been one of the main ports for Irish trade.

◄ **Tall Christian crosses** made of stone, stand out in the Irish countryside. Many of them are decorated with delicate carving. The images often tell a story from the Bible. The crosses are as much as 1,000 years old.

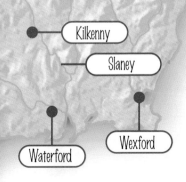

► **Castle** strongholds were built in Ireland by English invaders. Their soldiers were housed in these fortified buildings.

RELIGIONS

The Roman Catholic Church has had a powerful influence in Ireland. The Irish have always been a devout people, and priests play a very important part in their domestic and spiritual lives.

The ROMAN CATHOLIC church is very strong in Ireland. Most people in Ireland are Roman Catholics. More people go to church once a week in Ireland than in any other Christian country.

Ireland was one of the first countries in Europe to become Christian. When the Roman Empire fell and Europe plunged into the Dark Ages, Irish culture was kept alive by the monasteries. Ireland was called "the land of saints and scholars".

In Ireland, Catholic children are *confirmed* when they are twelve. In this ceremony children take on

When Ireland became Christian, stone crosses like this model were put up all over the countryside. Many are still standing today.

themselves the promises made for them at their baptism. A bishop touches their head to "confirm" that the Holy Spirit will help them to live a good life.

If people do wrong, they can go to church to *confess* their sins to a priest. He will issue a small punishment, such as saying a prayer called a *Hail Mary* over and over again. Once this has been done, the sinner is forgiven. Catholics have to go to confession at least once a year.

Priests are very important in Ireland. Catholic families like to boast that at least one family member has joined the church as a priest or a nun.

Roman Catholics belong to an international church. The spiritual leader of all the world's Catholics is the Pope, who lives in Rome. But Catholicism is not exactly the same all over the world.

There are many holy wells in Ireland, where people go to pray. Many were also holy in pre-Christian times.

Ireland is also home to many PROTESTANTS. In Ulster, made up of six counties in the northeast, Protestants are the majority. This part of Ireland is part of the United Kingdom. There is a very long history of trouble between the Catholic and Protestant groups in these six counties.

THE LITTLE PEOPLE

According to legend, there are *leprechauns*, or fairies, living in the Irish countryside. Leprechauns are small, grumpy shoemakers who guard hidden pots of gold. Treasure hunters can track them down by the sound of their shoemaker's hammer. But getting their gold is hard, as leprechauns are very cunning.

GREETINGS FROM **IRELAND!**

Irish is one of the oldest languages in Europe, but today English is the language most spoken in Ireland. This is because the English ruled Ireland for hundreds of years. Children who spoke Irish at school were often beaten or gagged. Today, children in the Republic have to learn Irish at school. This is now the official language, and the constitution is written in it.

The Irish are famous for their skill with words, or "blarney", as they call it. They are great storytellers. Some of the greatest poets and novelists in the English language have come from Ireland.

How do you say...

Hello
Dia is Muire ghuit

Goodbye
Beannacht dé leat

Thank you
Go raibh maith agat

Peace
Tsióchaín

7

CHRISTMAS

On December 25, Christians of the Roman Catholic and Protestant churches celebrate the birth of their saviour, Jesus Christ.

For all Christians the celebration of Christ's birth is one of the highlights of the religious year. The exact date of His birth is unknown, so Christmas takes place on the day on which, for thousands of years before Christianity, people celebrated the middle of winter.

In Ireland, *Advent* is a very important period of preparation for Christmas. Advent starts four Sundays before Christmas Day. In every church, four advent candles are placed on a stand. One candle is lit per week, until all four are burning.

By Christmas Eve, decorations have been put up. Holly and ivy is collected from the woods, and put up all over the house. Sprigs of mistletoe are hung from doorways for people to kiss under. And many people make small mangers like the one in which Jesus was born.

Throughout December, Advent candles are lit to herald the coming of Christmas.

Christmas Eve is a very frugal day, on which eating meat is forbidden. Late in the evening, families go to Midnight Mass, one of the most important church services in the Christian year.

Meanwhile, from every window, a red candle shines its light onto the street. This is to remember Mary and Joseph, who had to wander the Bethlehem streets because there was no room at the inn.

Long ago, the Irish believed that the Holy Family travelled the roads of Ireland every Christmas Eve. The candles were meant to light up their way.

Christmas Day is a time for families to share the best meal of the year. Many people dine on Spiced Beef. This old Irish dish takes a long time to prepare. Spices have to be rubbed into the meat twice a day for a week before it can be cooked.

After the mince pies, the *Christmas cake* is brought to the table. This is a very rich fruit cake. Then the meal is over. People tell stories and play games for the rest of the day.

This statuette shows the Holy Family when Jesus was a toddler. On Christmas Eve, candles are lit in their honour.

9

SAINT BRIGID

February 1 is the feast day of Saint Brigid, one of Ireland's two patron saints. Brigid was a nun who founded the first convent in Ireland. On Saint Brigid's Day people weave crosses from reeds. They are hung from doorways for good luck.

ONE FINE DAY when Saint Brigid was walking in the countryside, she came across a village. This village had no church, for its people still worshiped the old gods, and had not yet heard of Jesus Christ. The villagers were sad. The chief of their tribe was very ill. He lay dying in a small thatched hut in the center of the village.

Brigid went straight over to the dying chief's bedside. It saddened her to see anyone suffer that much. She felt his pain in her heart and wanted to do something to help him.

Brigid sat by the river that ran through the village. There she prayed to the Lord and asked Him to show mercy to the chief. She picked a bunch of reeds that were growing by the side of the river, and took them back to the chief's bedside.

Without saying a word, Brigid began to weave the reeds into a cross. As she was doing this, she prayed for the chief's salvation. When the cross was finished, the chief looked over to Brigid. He saw her serene face as she held the cross of reeds before him.

At that moment the chief saw a great white light. He saw the figure of Jesus Christ holding out His hands. It was the most amazing sight that he had ever seen.

The chief closed his eyes. He then said, "I have been saved by the Lord thanks to the prayers of Brigid." These were his dying words.

The villagers held a Christian funeral for the chief. They marked his grave with a stone cross. On it they placed the small cross of reeds woven by Brigid.

The villagers were very impressed with the kindness of Saint Brigid. They all gave up their old religion and converted to Christianity.

EASTER

Christians believe that Jesus died for all our sins.
On Easter Sunday, they celebrate His Resurrection,
when He rose from the dead.

The Resurrection of Jesus Christ, celebrated by Christians on Easter Sunday, is the most important part of the Christian faith.

Easter falls on the Sunday after the first full moon of spring. This full moon comes at a different time each year, so the date of Easter varies. It can happen at any point between March 22 and April 25.

The six weeks before Easter is called Lent. During Lent Christians remember the forty days that Jesus spent praying in

Hot cross buns are eaten on Good Friday. The cross symbolizes the crucifixion. On Easter Sunday, leek soup is a traditional dish.

the desert. People go hungry, or fast, just as Jesus did. If they are unable to do this, they give up one of their favourite things.

The week before Easter is called Holy Week. It starts with Palm Sunday, the day on which Jesus rode into Jerusalem on a donkey. On this day there are processions all over Ireland.

Jesus was crucified on Good Friday. This is a special day of prayer and fasting.

On Easter Saturday people go to church. They light small candles off the "Paschal candle" that has been blessed by

The Rosary is a set of prayers. People use Rosary beads to help them keep count. There is one bead for each prayer.

the priest. Then the darkened church is filled with hundreds of tiny lights. Candles are an important part of Easter, as Jesus is often said to be "The Light of the World".

Easter Sunday is a quiet day, spent at home with the family. Children are given eggs to paint, and everyone enjoys the first good meal after Lent – often a roasted spring lamb.

Eggs and chicks are important symbols of Christ's Resurrection. In parts of Ireland people build little "Easter houses". These are filled with coloured eggs, which are rolled down hills before being eaten.

SAINT PATRICK'S DAY

Saint Patrick converted the Irish to Christianity. On March 17 Irish people all over the world celebrate the feast day of their patron saint.

Irish people can be found all over the world. This is mainly because of the most tragic event in Irish history – the Great Famine of 1845. At the time most people could only afford to eat potatoes. When the potato crop failed, over a million people died. Millions more were forced to leave Ireland to build new lives abroad, mostly in the United States.

Saint Patrick is one of Ireland's patron saints. He wears green, the colour of the Irish countryside.

Ireland has been a poor country until quite recently. Many people have had to leave in order to find work. Today there are more people of Irish descent living abroad than there are people in Ireland itself.

Saint Patrick's Day is celebrated all over the world. Wherever there are Irish people, March 17 is celebrated with traditional Irish food and folk music. Many towns and cities hold huge parades, led by brass bands.

People pin sprigs of *shamrock*, Ireland's national emblem, on their clothes. This is because Saint Patrick used the three-leaved plant to describe the Christian belief that God has three aspects: the Father, the Son and the Holy Spirit.

In Chicago, a city which has a large Irish population, green dye is poured into the river. This colour is especially associated with Ireland. Ireland has such a high rainfall that it is one of the greenest places in the world.

In Ireland itself Saint Patrick's Day is an important religious festival. Some towns hold parades, but in most parts of Ireland it is a quiet day, spent at home with family and friends.

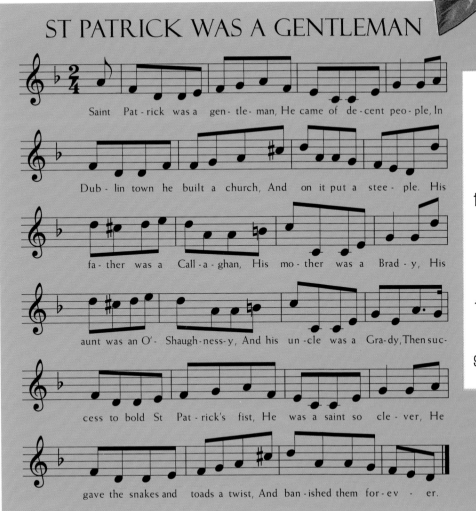

ST PATRICK WAS A GENTLEMAN

Saint Pat-rick was a gen-tle-man, He came of de-cent peo-ple, In Dub-lin town he built a church, And on it put a stee-ple. His fa-ther was a Call-a-ghan, His mo-ther was a Brad-y, His aunt was an O'- Shaugh-ness-y, And his un-cle was a Gra-dy, Then suc-cess to bold St Pat-rick's fist, He was a saint so cle-ver, He gave the snakes and toads a twist, And ban-ished them for-ev - er.

This traditional song is often played on Saint Patrick's Day. It tells how Saint Patrick banished all the snakes and toads from Ireland. It is true that Ireland has no snakes. The reason for this, according to the legend, is that Saint Patrick cast them into the sea using his bishop's staff.

SAINT PATRICK

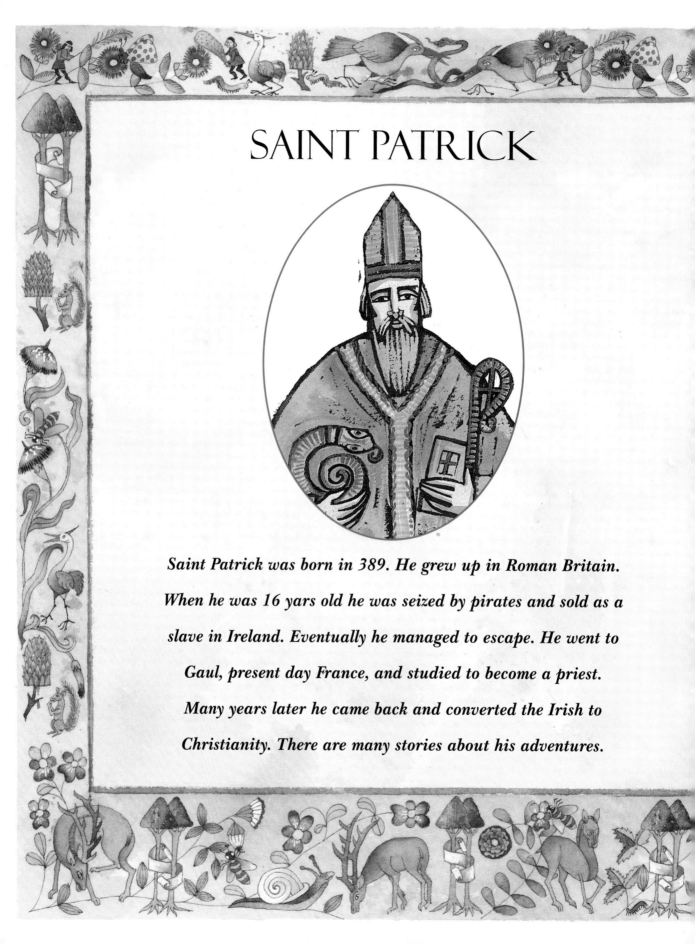

Saint Patrick was born in 389. He grew up in Roman Britain. When he was 16 yars old he was seized by pirates and sold as a slave in Ireland. Eventually he managed to escape. He went to Gaul, present day France, and studied to become a priest. Many years later he came back and converted the Irish to Christianity. There are many stories about his adventures.

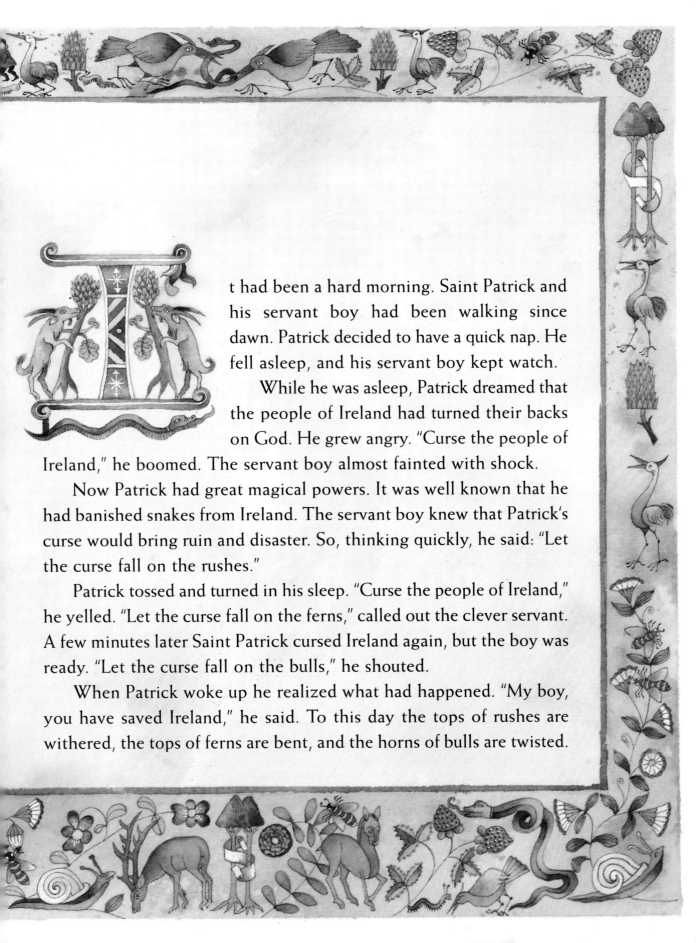

It had been a hard morning. Saint Patrick and his servant boy had been walking since dawn. Patrick decided to have a quick nap. He fell asleep, and his servant boy kept watch.

While he was asleep, Patrick dreamed that the people of Ireland had turned their backs on God. He grew angry. "Curse the people of Ireland," he boomed. The servant boy almost fainted with shock.

Now Patrick had great magical powers. It was well known that he had banished snakes from Ireland. The servant boy knew that Patrick's curse would bring ruin and disaster. So, thinking quickly, he said: "Let the curse fall on the rushes."

Patrick tossed and turned in his sleep. "Curse the people of Ireland," he yelled. "Let the curse fall on the ferns," called out the clever servant. A few minutes later Saint Patrick cursed Ireland again, but the boy was ready. "Let the curse fall on the bulls," he shouted.

When Patrick woke up he realized what had happened. "My boy, you have saved Ireland," he said. To this day the tops of rushes are withered, the tops of ferns are bent, and the horns of bulls are twisted.

HOW TO MAKE A POTATO STAMP BOOK

The Irish have a great love of books. Make your own and stamp its cover with a potato print.

Once you have made a cover, why not write a story to go inside? Copy it carefully into the book, then illustrate it with more potato prints.

Potatoes form a large part of the Irish diet. They are used in many traditional dishes. A favourite is colcannon, a mix of hot mashed potato, cabbage, butter and milk.

YOU WILL NEED
One large potato
A kitchen knife
Water-based paint
Several sheets of white A4 paper
Thick coloured A4 paper
A craft needle
Thin ribbon

3 To make the stamp, get an adult to help you. Cut the potato in half lengthways. Carve the shamrock shape into the potato as shown above. Dip into paint and stamp on the cover.

1 To make the book, lay out several sheets of white paper on top of one sheet of coloured paper for the cover. Fold in half to make a book shape. With the needle make four equally spaced small holes through all thicknesses of the fold.

2 From top to bottom, the holes are numbered 1, 2, 3 and 4. Starting from the cover, thread the ribbon through the holes in this order: 2, 1, 2, 3, 4, 3. Tie the ends of the ribbon in a bow to bind the book.

LAMMAS DAY

In August farmers bring crafts, food and livestock to the Lammas fairs, which take place all over Ireland.

Many Irish men wear tweed caps like the one above, especially in the countryside. Irish tweeds are famed for their quality. Below is some dulse, an edible seaweed regarded in Ireland as a great delicacy.

Lammas day is a Christian harvest festival. It falls on August 1, and over the following month many Irish towns hold Lammas fairs, where farmers can come and sell their produce.

One of the most famous fairs is held in Ballycastle, in County Antrim, on the last Monday and Tuesday of August.

Many things are sold at the Ballycastle Lammas Fair. *Dulse*, a type of edible seaweed, is very popular. Another speciality is *Yellowman*, a kind of sweet, crumbly toffee. And many stalls sell the tweed caps and clothes that northern Ireland is famous for.

Ballycastle is also a horse market. Horses are very important in

STEAK SANDWICH

MAKES 1

Butter for spreading, softened
2 thick slices bread
1 tsp vegetable oil
1 minute steak, about 250g
Mustard

1 Butter bread slices on one side.
2 Heat oil in a large frying pan over medium heat. Add steak and cook 3 minutes. Use a fork to turn steak over. Cook 1 to 3 minutes, or longer, until it is done as you like it.

3 Put steak on one piece of the bread and spread with mustard. Top with the remaining bread and press together.

Ireland. Because of its moist climate, Ireland has excellent pasture land for grazing. As a result, Ireland has some of Europe's best racehorses. Racing is a very popular sport. It has a long history in Ireland. The ancient Celts, the ancestors of the modern Irish, were famous for their horsemanship.

The steeplechase, a type of race in which horses have to jump over fences, was invented when two Irishmen had a race to the local church, jumping over hedges and ditches on their way. It is Ireland's most popular type of horseracing.

PUCK FAIR

Every summer thousands of people descend on the quiet town of Killorglin, in southwest Ireland. They come to sell horses, swap stories and play music.

On August 2 Gypsies from all over the country visit the fair in Killorglin, a town in County Kerry. The Gypsies are a very small group, but they do have their own language, *Shanty*. They believe that their ancestors were the roving bards, or singing poets, of ancient Ireland.

Today most Gypsies live in one place. But they used to roam the countryside in carts, stopping in villages to earn their living.

The Gypsies dress differently from most Irish people. Women wear long plaid shawls like the doll on the left. To the right is a model carousel. Many fairground amusements like this can be found at the Puck Fair.

TRADITIONAL SODA BREAD

MAKES ONE LOAF

*Vegetable oil for greasing
700g plain flour
2 tsp baking powder
1 tsp bicarbonate of soda
1 tsp salt
1 egg, lightly beaten
300ml buttermilk*

1 Heat oven to 190°C/375°F/ Gas 5. Lightly grease a baking sheet with oil.

2 Put dry ingredients in a bowl and stir. Beat egg and buttermilk together. Add to flour and mix to make a soft dough.

3 Knead dough until smooth. Pat into a ball. Place on baking sheet. Cut an X in top.

4 Bake 30 to 40 minutes until bottom sounds hollow when you tap it. Let cool 15 minutes. Serve warm.

The festival lasts for three days. On the evening of the first day a billy goat, his horns decorated with ribbons and a crown, is paraded through the streets. King Puck, as he is known, is then enthroned on a three-storey platform in the town square. He stays there for the whole festival, looking down on the celebration below.

One tale has it that this custom celebrates the time when a herd of goats saved the town from Cromwell's army. They ran into

DANNY BOY

Oh Dan-ny Boy, the pipes, the pipes are call-ing From glen to glen, and down the moun-tain side; The sum-mer's gone, and all the ro-ses fad-ing, 'Tis you, 'tis you must go, and I must bide. But come ye back when sum-mer's in the mea-dow, Or when the val-ley's hushed and white with snow; And I'll be here in sun-shine or in sha-dow, Oh, Dan-ny Boy, oh, Dan-ny Boy, I love you so!

Danny Boy is a popular Irish ballad. It was first sung nearly 150 years ago, although the melody is much older. Its theme — that of seeing loved ones leave home — is close to the Irish heart. Danny Boy is the song of a woman whose beloved is going off to war. The pipes in the song belong to military bands that are marching through the glens, or valleys, picking up recruits.

Killorglin, warning the locals that the English army was on its way. This gave them enough time to defend the town.

On the second day farmers take their cattle to the market. Shops, cafés and pubs are open all night. People dance to the music of violins, or fiddles, as they are called in Ireland. They play fast tunes known as jigs and reels, accompanied by the low beat of the *bodhran*, the Irish drum.

On the third day, when everyone is quite exhausted, King Puck is taken down from his throne. The fair is over until next year.

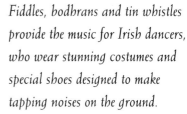

Fiddles, bodhrans and tin whistles provide the music for Irish dancers, who wear stunning costumes and special shoes designed to make tapping noises on the ground.

25

HOW TO MAKE A TWEED GOAT

Use one of Ireland's most ancient fabrics to make your very own King Puck.

Tweed has as long history in Ireland. Centuries ago when the country was divided between lots of different tribes, tweed served a very important purpose. Each tribe had its own type of tweed, with its own distinctive colour and weave. This meant that when tribes went into battle, their warriors could recognize each other. The Irish tribes no longer exist, but there are still many different types of tweed, all made in different parts of the country. Some people still wear their local tweed with pride. Irish tweed is now sold all over the world and is renowned for its very high quality.

YOU WILL NEED

Tracing paper
Tweed fabric
Needle and thread
Coloured ribbons
A pipe cleaner
Cotton wool
Coloured wool

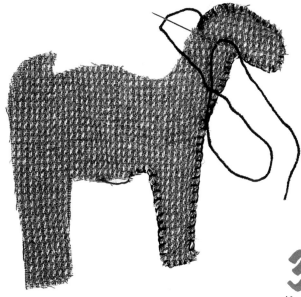

1 Trace the goat's body and ears onto tracing paper. Pin paper onto double layer of tweed. Cut the shapes. To sew body shapes together, start at the tummy. Use blanket stitch. Push needle through tweed, so thread loops over edge. Push needle through loop of thread then back into tweed. Repeat process. Leave gap for stuffing.

3 With one of the coloured ribbons tie a bow around the goat's neck. Decorate the body with more ribbons. If you want to hang the goat up, attach one length of ribbon to either end of its back.

2 Fill the whole goat with cotton wool. Sew up the gap and sew a line of stitching up the legs. Blanket stitch around the ears and stitch onto the goat. Stitch its nose, beard, eyes and tail with coloured wool. Bend the pipe cleaner into a U-shape. Stitch on top of the goat's head to make horns.

ALL SOULS' DAY

On November 2 people remember dead family members. They spend the day by their loved ones' gravesides and pray for their souls.

In all Catholic countries, the *last rites* are given to people before they die. A priest comes to their bedside and they take *Holy Communion* for the last time.

Holy Communion is Christianity's main ceremony. It comes from the Last Supper, when Jesus asked His disciples to remember Him by sharing bread and wine. Catholics believe that when a person eats the wafer given to them during Holy Communion, it turns into the body of Jesus Christ.

After people die, their loved ones pray for their souls to reach heaven. All Souls' Day is a special time to say these prayers.

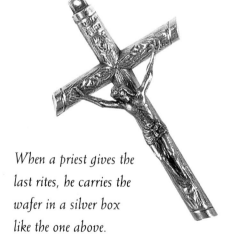

When a priest gives the last rites, he carries the wafer in a silver box like the one above.

All Souls' Day was started in France, long ago, by Saint Odile. He had the idea when he was celebrating All Saints' Day, which falls on November 1.

All Saints' Day was set aside by the Church for all of its saints. Saint Odile was a very kind man. He thought that ordinary people needed the prayers of the Church much more than the saints. So he started the custom of praying for the souls of all the other people who have died on the next day.

In Ireland All Saints' Day is a day to spend time with the family.

Above is Mary, known in Ireland as "Our Lady". Below, from left to right, are Saint Stephen, Saint Francis and Saint Anthony.

Everyone eats a big meal, and children play apple bobbing. In this game, apples floating in a tub of water have to be picked out with the teeth. It is a lot more difficult than it may sound!

The next day, All Souls', is a day of fasting. Families spend the day at the graves of their loved ones. Then they go to church and pray for the souls of their dead relatives.

In the past people thought that souls of the dead came to visit their old homes on All Souls' night. Families would leave the door unlatched and lay a place at the table for each dead member of the family.

OTHER IMPORTANT FESTIVALS

Although more and more people are choosing to live in towns, Ireland is still strong in its rural ways. The countryside is very rich in customs and festivals.

Single people wear the Claddagh *ring with the crown facing inwards. When they find true love, they turn the crown to face outward.*

SHROVE TUESDAY is the traditional day to get married in rural Ireland. This is because it comes just before Lent, a time during which marriage was forbidden. People came to think that anyone who did not get married at this time did not intend to that year. Unmarried people who did not marry then were frowned upon. In some parts of Ireland the Sunday following Shrove Tuesday was known as "Chalk Sunday". People who were still unmarried then had their clothes decorated with chalk marks by young boys and girls.

MICHAELMAS falls on September 29. On this day the custom is to eat a Michaelmas goose. Michaelmas is seen as the last day of summer. Around this time, farmers can be seen driving herds of cattle to their winter quarters. Cattle are very important in a rural country like Ireland. Because of Ireland's very high rainfall, there is plenty of rich pasture land for them to graze on.

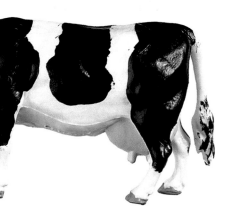

Cows play a vital role in rural life. Dairy products are a major money earner for Irish farmers. This is a model of a Friesian milk cow.

WORDS TO KNOW

Baptism: The ceremony in which someone is admitted into the Christian faith.

Bard: A singing poet and storyteller.

Billy goat: A male goat.

Celts: An ancient European people, the ancestors of the Irish, the Scottish and the Welsh.

Cromwell, Oliver: An English soldier, ruler of England from 1649 to 1658, who led an invading army into Ireland in 1649.

Dark Ages: A period that started about AD 490, when the Roman Empire, which had controlled most of Europe, much of the Middle East and North Africa, collapsed. For the next 500 years the prosperity brought by Roman rule was lost, leaving Europe in the Dark Ages.

Frugal: Avoiding waste. Careful and sparing.

Holy Communion: A Christian ritual that commemorates the Last Supper of Jesus Christ.

Mass: The Roman Catholic service in which the ritual of Holy Communion takes place.

Paschal: Related to Easter.

Patron saint: A saint who watches over a particular group. Nations, towns and professions all have patron saints.

Protestant: A member of one of the Protestant churches, which together form one of the main branches of Christianity. The Protestants split from the Roman Catholic Church in the sixteenth century.

Roman Catholic: A member of the Roman Catholic Church, the largest branch of Christianity. The head of this church is the Pope.

Saint: A title given to very holy people by some Christian churches. Saints are important in the Roman Catholic Church.

Wafer: A thin, round piece of unrisen bread that is used in Holy Communion.

ACKNOWLEDGMENTS

WITH THANKS TO:

Articles of Faith, Bury cross p6, Holy Family p8-9, crucifix, rosary p12-13, wafer box, crucifix p28-29. Catholic Truth Society, London St Patrick p14, medallions p19. Pollock's Toy Museum, London gypsy, donkey, wagon, horses p20-23, The Vintage House, London carousel p23, Joe Hughes musical instruments, dress, shoes p24-25. Elm Tree Pub, Oxford bodhran p25.

PHOTOGRAPHS BY:

All photographs by Bruce Mackie except: John Elliott p21(top).
Cover photograph by Katie Vandyck.

ILLUSTRATIONS BY:

Fiona Saunders title page, p4-5, Mountain High Maps ® Copyright © 1993 Digital Wisdom, Inc. p4-5. Tracy Rich p7. Robert Shadbolt p11. Alison Fleming p16, Susan Moxley (border) p16-17.

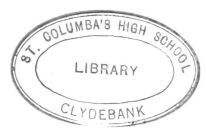
INDEX